D1134950

COLLEGE OF MARIN LIBRARY
KENTFIELD, CALIFORNIA

REVISED EDITION

REDWOOD EMPIRE
WILDFLOWER JEWELS

By Dorothy King Young

*   *   *   *   *   *   *   *

Edited by Vinson Brown

*   *   *   *   *   *   *   *

Copyright 1964, 1970, by Dorothy King Young

Cover picture by Charles Young

<u>Calypso</u> <u>bulbosa</u> or Redwood Orchid

COLLEGE OF MARIN LIBRARY
KENTFIELD. CALIFORNIA

Scarlet Pimpernel

SBN 911010-56-4 - paper
SBN 911010-57-2 - cloth

Published by Naturegraph Publishers, Healdsburg, California

NATUREGRAPH PRESS

2

TABLE OF CONTENTS

THIS BOOK IS DEDICATED TO:
The Kings everywhere, and
to the Misses Helen and Beulah Gilkey,
who led me onto the happy path of botany.

California Native Plant Society proudly
lines up with the Sierra Club and the
Audubon Society in preserving our
beautiful environment.

THE JOY OF THE JEWELS

Jewels! The very word brings to mind the glowing, shimmering beauty, the translucent loveliness of diamonds, rubies and pearls. SUGARSTICKS are, indeed, the jewels supreme of the Redwood Empire, but LADYSLIPPERS, CALYPSOS, GROUNDCONES, PHANTOM ORCHIDS, FALSE PINK ASPARAGUS and the PYROLAS also have moments of indescribable elegance.

Fifty years of pleasant searching for wildflower beauties of the forest, the mountain meadows, and the seashore would fill, many times over, the pages presented here. Rather it is our hope that the lovely flower pictures, the general times when each may be found, and a few specific locations may whet your appetite for discoveries and written records of your own. "Finders-keepers" may be safely played with your camera.

If you have leanings toward building a natural wildflower garden in your yard be sure to plant your lilies, clintonia, ginger and redwood sorrel in a deer-proof enclosure. We secured permission from the owners to hike the nearby logging roads to look for plants already partly mangled and those in the path of immediate destruction. Several fine clintonia and lily specimens were planted here on the trails and meadows of GRANDPA CHARLEY'S PARK, our own little mountain ranch near the lively coast town of Gualala at the extreme southern end of Mendocino County, California. Naturally we watched them almost daily to see if they would perk up. Some even were on the verge of blooming. Imagine our consternation upon returning from a trip to find the buds neatly clipped off as well as most of the leaves. Dusk brought the culprits into full view, a beautiful doe and her twin fawns. The deer are too precious and trusting to be disturbed, so now we put the things we know they will eat in our fenced orchard.

Many of our wildflower jewels have already become relatively scarce and some may even be in danger of vanishing, so:

DON'T TRAMPLE OR DESTROY;
DO TREASURE AND ENJOY!

HOW TO USE THIS BOOK

Were it financially possible to produce a handbook of ALL our wildflowers in full color that would retail at a reasonable price, we would do it. "One picture is worth a thousand words" is as true in this modern space age as when the Chinese sage spoke it. But we still cannot print in color economically enough to do more than part of our wildflowers in their shining glory at a price anybody can afford to pay.

We have pictured nearly all of the still plentiful roadside beauties, as many as we can spare to a family, a few really rare jewels, and have left space for you to record YOUR findings. You should see the Young's field botany books! Margins are filled with notes of when, where, why, and whatever. Tacked on the wall of our favorite mountain house on Big Rock Ranch, Orleans, Humboldt County, we've kept long lists of botanical discoveries, year by year. In the interests of good housekeeping and on account of summertime spatters from cooking, these records have been destroyed. So keep your records in your own book so that you can compare them as the years go by. Imagine my own pleasure when I found a grandnephew's flower record tacked up alongside of mine!

Don't shy away from learning the scientific names. True they are not easy, but they are accepted, the world over. Sure, the eminent botanists don't always agree, but basically they are seeking to simplify our knowledge and make botany more complete and correct. Study the next four pages carefully before you start using the picture section and learn the plant parts and forms, then study the habitats (page 8). At the back of the book on page 73 you will find help in identifying many of the flowers you meet by color. Learn to supplement your knowledge from one or more of the truly scientific books that are listed in the bibliography on page 79. When you start using the color pictures and the descriptions to identify the flowers you see, remember to study and compare everything most carefully, as it is easy to make mistakes since some flowers of different species are very similar.

Keep looking and seeking. There is a lifetime in front of you of fun and joy if you become really a wildflower fan!

CLASSIFICATION OF FLOWERS

This book is a popular introduction to wildflowers of the Redwood Empire and is not meant to be a technical reference to complete classification. The more complete books are listed in the bibliography on page 79. Nevertheless this book can be used to classify all the plants described and pictured in its pages if careful use is made of both pictures and descriptions. To help you understand the names of flower parts, flower types, inflorescences (the way flowers are arranged on a plant) and the different types of leaves, the pictures on the next two pages will help you. Study these pictures carefully and learn the names so you will recognize and understand what the descriptions are talking about in the main part of the book.

The plant families in this book are not arranged in the way botanists usually organize them, but are placed in alphabetical order for ease of use by a beginner. In a sense this book can be thought of as a telephone directory to the more beautiful and interesting flowers of the Redwood Empire, with the family name being the prefix.

Unfortunately botanists themselves are far from complete agreement as to the scientific arrangement of plant families. We like best Dr. Leroy Abrams magnificent four volumes on an ILLUSTRATED FLORA OF THE PACIFIC STATES, which has the families arranged as follows:

Phylum PTERIDOPHYTA - Ferns.
Phylum SPERMATOPHYTA - Seed Plants.
    Class GYMNOSPERMAE - Cone-bearing Plants.
        Families: Taxaceae (Yews), Pinaceae (pines and firs), Taxodiaceae (Redwoods), etc.
    Class ANGIOSPERMAE - Flowering Plants.
        Sub-class MONOCOTYLEDONAE - Parallel-veined.
            Families: Typhaceae (Cat-tails), Sparganiaceae (Bur-reeds), Potamogetonaceae (Pondweeds), etc.
        Sub-class DICOTYLEDONAE - Net-veined Plants.
            Families: Sauraceae (Lizard's-tail Family), Salicaceae (Willows), etc., and ending with Compositae (Sunflowers).

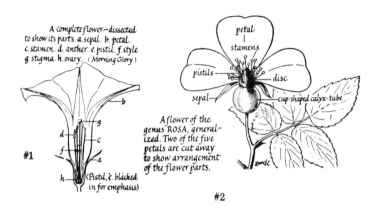

#1

A complete flower–dissected to show its parts. a. sepal. b. petal. c. stamen. d. anther. e. pistil. f. style g. stigma. h. ovary. (Morning Glory)

(Pistil, 'e' blacked in for emphasis)

A flower of the genus ROSA, generalized. Two of the five petals are cut away to show arrangement of the flower parts.

#2

#1 and #2.   <u>Two typical flowers</u>, showing the names of their parts.

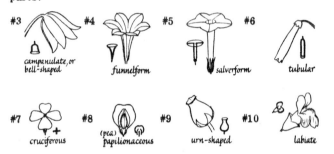

#3 campanulate, or bell-shaped

#4 funnelform

#5 salverform

#6 tubular

#7 cruciferous

#8 (pea) papilionaceous

#9 urn-shaped

#10 labiate

#3 to #10.   <u>Types of Flowers</u>. #3 and #4 are <u>apetalous</u>, which means without distinct petals and sepals; #7 and #8 are <u>choripetalous</u>, which means the petals and sepals are each completely free from each other; #5, 6, 9 and 10 are <u>sympetalous</u>, which means the petals and sepals are all more or less closely joined together.

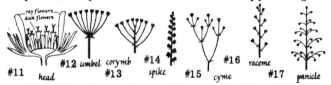

#11 head   #12 umbel   corymb #13   #14 spike   #15 cyme   #16 raceme   #17 panicle

#11 to #17.   <u>Types of flower formations</u>. The daisy and sunflower look like single flowers, but really are heads of flowers (#11).

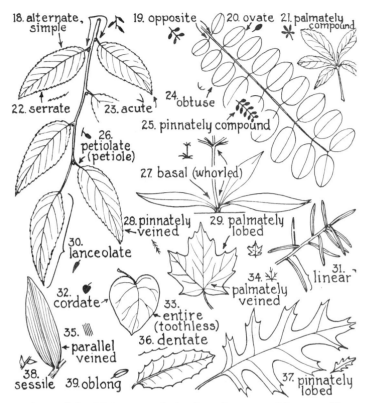

18. alternate, simple
19. opposite
20. ovate
21. palmately compound
22. serrate
23. acute
24. obtuse
25. pinnately compound
26. petiolate (petiole)
27. basal (whorled)
28. pinnately veined
29. palmately lobed
30. lanceolate
31. linear
32. cordate
33. entire (toothless)
34. palmately veined
35. parallel veined
36. dentate
37. pinnately lobed
38. sessile
39. oblong

#18 to #39. Main types of simple and compound leaves. The small figure that is beside each big one shows the generalized shape from which every leaf form shown takes its name. Thus, dentate means toothlike and serrate means saw-like; cordate means heart-shaped and linear means like a line; sessile means the leaf has no stem or is stemless; while petiolate means the leaf has a short stem or petiole.

* * * * *

(NOTE: the pictures shown on these two pages have been adapted from the book, THE AMATEUR NATURALIST'S HANDBOOK, by Vinson Brown, with the kind permission of the author and the publishers, Little, Brown and Company, of Boston, Massachusetts.)

HABITATS OR PLANT COMMUNITIES

A habitat and a plant community may be considered synonymous in this book. Just as human beings form communities in their cities and towns, so plants form communities of associated plants. For the identification of the flowers as described and pictured in this book, a knowledge of the habitats in which each is found is often very important. You will notice that each plant described in this book has the habitats in which it is found listed along the side of the page. When looking for such a plant, watch for it in the correct habitats. The habitats and their abbreviations (if needed) appear below.

Beach - is a community of plants living along the ocean shore where they are subject to salt spray and winds and often have to dwell in sand. Also called Sand.

Brush - is also called Northern Coastal Scrub and Chaparral, and is made up mainly of bushes, some with stiff branches, and many with small leaves to resist the heat.

Coniferous Forest (Conif.) - is the forest dominated by either the redwoods or the Douglas Fir, with the forest floor carpeted thickly by the needles of these and similar trees.

Cultivated and Urban (Cultiv.) - includes farms, orchards, parks, towns, cities, etc.

Grassland (Grass) - is found in the lowland valleys and hills wherever grass is the predominant kind of plant.

Hardwood Forests (Hardwd.) - These forests are generally found nearer the coast than the Oak Forests, and often are found to take over temporarily land where Coniferous Forests have been burned. The predominant trees are tanbark oaks, madrone and bay or laurel trees.

Marsh - includes both fresh water marshes and swamps.

Meadow - Higher in the hills and mountains grassy meadows are often found surrounded by coniferous forest.

Most Habitats (Most Hab.) - is a term used when a plant is found in many different habitats.

Oak Woodlands (Oak) - includes woods in which oak trees, such as the Black and Live Oaks, are predominant.

Rocks - means rocky areas, cliffs, etc.

Savanna (Sav.) - is a grassland with scattered trees.

Streamside Woodland (Str.Wd.) - woods along streams.

Water - includes streams, rivers, ponds and lakes.

INTRODUCTION TO COLOR PLATES

Except for the first two pictures in this color plate section, all the pictures show individual species of wild flowers, taken especially to aid in their identification as well as to give an appreciation of their beauty.

1. BOOK AND JEWELS. These beautiful forest jewels and rare flowers were gathered by Grandpa Charley and me from areas in the Redwood Empire that were being destroyed by loggers and others. Replanted, they were saved and then shared with herbariums up and down the coast where the exclamations of the viewers showed that many a professional botanist had never seen these rare gems together before. All of these, heaths, anemones, wall flowers, groundcones, coral root and phantom orchid, are mysterious children of the woods that we describe and picture later in more detail, but are here shown gathered in one glorious cluster.

2. CALYPSOS (Redwood Orchids) and REDWOOD VIO- Conif. LETS spread a royal carpet, seemingly decked with fairy lanterns that beckon and twinkle in the filtered shade where, indeed, many miniature creatures of our woodlands might actually be holding forth. Near this forest sanctuary are aisles carefully laid out and marked with sword ferns, trilliums, and the brightly shining, heart-shaped leaves of wild ginger (6), which invite you to step gently and watch tenderly. Picture taken near Gualala, Mendocino County.

ARUM FAMILY   ARACEAE

3. YELLOW SKUNK CABBAGE, Lysichiton americanum, usually grows under trees like alders, which are commonly Brush Conif. associated with swamps, marshes, stream banks.   Bruise Water one of the huge leaves to find out how it got its name.   1 1/2 Marsh to 3 ft. tall.   Early spring.
First found_____Where_____

BARBERRY FAMILY   BERBERIDACEAE

4. OREGON GRAPE, Mahonia nervosa, is found through- Conif. out the Redwood Empire.   It has special significance in our

10

1. Jewels of the Forest
(Photo by Charles Young)

2. Fairy Lights in Redwoods
(Photo by Charles Young)

3. Skunk Cabbage
(Photo by Frank Kemp)

4. Oregon Grape
(Photo by E. F. Jewett)

5. Vanilla Leaf
(Photo by Alice Ackley)

6. Wild Ginger
(Photo by Frank Kemp)

8. Hound's Tongue
(Photo by Frank Kemp)

Groundcones
oto by Lula Barnes)

7. Dutchman's Pipe
(Photo by E. F. Jewett)

10. Purple Ruffles
(Photo by Louise Hallberg)

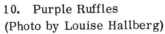

Empire's northernmost fringe in Josephine County, Oregon, since it is closely related to Oregon's state flower, <u>Berberis aquifolium</u>. The glossy, green leaves with their spiny edges remind us of holly. 1 to 3 ft. high.
First found_____Where_____

Conif.

5. VANILLA LEAF, <u>Achlys triphylla</u> (also called Sweet-after-Death and Deer Foot). It has three unusually shaped leaflets at the top of a wiry stem where they spread out like an opened umbrella. The white flowers crowd together at the spike-like end of the flower stem which rises directly from the root cluster, aloof from the leaves. 10-15" high.
First found_____Where_____

BIRTHWORT FAMILY   ARISTOLOCHIACEAE

Conif.
Oak
Hardw.

6. WILD GINGER, <u>Asarum caudatum</u>, hugs the forest floor like a spicy rug near pools and seeps. The strangely shaped, dark red flowers have three long, tapering lobes; the heart-shaped leaves are shiny green above and red beneath. 3-4" high. Another variety (Hartweg's Ginger), has beautifully-shaped white-veined leaves; at higher altitudes.
First found_____Where_____

Str. Wd.

7. DUTCHMAN'S PIPE, <u>Aristolochia californica</u> (California Pipe Vine), is a twiner or climber with pendulous, greenish to purple, bowl-shaped flowers. 9-13' long.
First found_____Where_____

BORAGE FAMILY   BORAGINACEAE

Oak
Str. Wd.
Chap.

8. HOUND'S TONGUE, <u>Cynoglossum grande</u>, is found in filtered shade, usually protected by scattered shrubs or trees. A large perennial (1 to 3' high) from a heavy root; the blooms are like big forget-me-nots, exquisitely blue, borne in a loose cluster (panicle) at the top of the plant.
First found_____Where_____

BROOMRAPE FAMILY   OROBANCHACEAE

Most
Hab.

9. GROUNDCONE, <u>Boschniakia strobilacea</u>, is really a beautiful robber, since it is attached through a corm-like

basal thickening to the root of its host, a madrone or manzanita. We have run across these strange parasitic growths
the full length of the Redwood Empire clear north to Ash-
land, Oregon.   Groundcone is exactly as pictured: thick,
burgundy-brown as it comes through the ground, each point
developing into a soft beige, star-like blossom, which, as
the summer progresses, turns into a fat, shining, ruby-red,
translucent JEWEL.   You will thrill anew at the wonders of
earth when you find your first groundcone. 4-10"; Apr.-July.
First found_____Where_____

10. PURPLE RUFFLES, Orobanche grayana, var. viola-
ceae, is still another beautiful robber. Apparently the seeds
germinate and the rootlet attaches itself to the root of the
host, the gum plant (Grindelia) as it grows on wet, sandy
beaches.   We have seen several specimens of this striking
parasitic plant as they lay on the sand near the host after
being kicked out of their snug resting place by the feet of
children in Alder Creek State Park. 2-4" tall.
First found_____Where_____

Beach

BUCKTHORN FAMILY   RHAMNACEAE

11. CALIFORNIA LILAC or REDWOOD COAST CEANO-
THUS, Ceanothus gloriosus, var. exaltatus, answers to many
other common names, such as Blueblossom, Tick Brush, and
Blue Brush. It grows in masses along roads in the foothills
and literally "takes over" in the uncultivated areas, cloaking
the countryside with misty blue for miles. Common throughout the coastal mountain regions from March on in appealing
bloom.   There are many varieties. Up to 10' tall.
First found_____Where_____

Chap.
Oak

12. WHITETHORN, Ceanothus incanus, is sometimes
called white California Lilac, as the feathery plumes do re-
semble their cultivated "cousins" somewhat.   The sharp,
thorn-like branches try to catch you as you pass through the
brush.   The flowers are soft and branch freely in dense,
compound panicles. This bush is often numerous and is one
reason why chaparral is so hard to go through. 6-10' tall.
First found_____Where_____

Chap.
Str. Wd.

14

11. Redwood Coast Ceanothus
(Photo by Charles Young)

12. Whitethorn
(Photo by Frank Kemp)

13. Dune Buckwheat
(Photo by Gordon McBride)

14. Western Windflower
(Photo by E. F. Jewett)

15. Crimson Columbine
(Photo by Lula Barnes)

16. Blue Larkspur
(Photo by E. F. Jewett)

17a. Scarlet Larkspur
(Photo by Lula Barnes)

17b. Scarlet Larkspur
(Photo by Wayne Roderick)

18. Pacific Dogwood
(Photo by Violet Wooden)

BUCKWHEAT FAMILY   POLYGONACEAE

Beach

13. DUNE BUCKWHEAT, Eriogonum latifolium, clings to the dunes and steep banks, always buffed by windy gusts from the sea. Perhaps the Greek interpretation of the word Eriogonum - woolly knees - has real significance for this particular buckwheat in its coastal form, as it is very hairy. The flowers appear in head-like clusters. 1-2" high.
First found_____Where_____

BUTTERCUP or CROWFOOT FAMILY RANUNCULACEAE

Buttercups, next to dandelions, are probably the best known flowering plants in the world. But, do you recognize these other members of the vast buttercup family?

Oak
Conif.

14. WESTERN WINDFLOWER, Anemone deltoidea (Western Wood Anemone), delights in lightly shaded spots in the mixed redwood forest. Each slender stem has three notched leaves about halfway up to the solitary, white flower that nods to you in the slightest breeze. 4-12" high.
First found_____Where_____

Conif.
Oak

15. CRIMSON COLUMBINE, Aquilegia formosa, is a strikingly beautiful perennial frequently seen on road banks and woodsy edges of meadows. It has light green leaves that accent the nodding pale scarlet-petaled trumpets. The spurs contain much nectar for hummingbirds. The leaves form two sets of three leaflets. 1 1/2-3 1/2' high.
First found_____Where_____

Grass
Brush

16. BLUE LARKSPUR, Delphinium decorum, shows how well plants adapt to their environments. This stocky beauty is able to resist the coastal winds while similar relatives of the mountain swales and gullies are taller and more graceful. Leaves and stems covered with small hairs. 4-12" high.
First found_____Where_____

Brush
Oak
Conif.

17. SCARLET LARKSPUR, Delphinium nudicaule, is a flaming beauty. The oddly shaped bells or horns are daintier and more widely spaced than in the above flower, and the lower petal is cleft to about the middle. 8-32" high.
First found_____Where_____

DOGWOOD FAMILY   CORNACEAE

18. MOUNTAIN DOGWOOD, Cornus nuttallii, often attains the height and stature of a tree, but the slender limbs, when clothed in their six inch, saucer-like blooms, look like Conif. Str. Wd. a huge, well-arranged bouquet. Actually the blooms are the center cluster, but they are surrounded by the large, lustrous-white bracts, which appear to be petals. Sometimes called Pacific Dogwood. Twigs become dark red. 12-30'.
First found_____Where_____

EVENING PRIMROSE FAMILY   ONAGRACEAE

19 & 20. RED RIBBONS or LOVELY CLARKIA, Clarkia concinna (or Fringed Clarkia), likes to be neighborly on Conif. Rocks banks and bluffs where great colonies are seen splashing their rosy-pink cascades over the drying landscape.   They glorify many a dry cliff-side from June on.   The flowers appear in the axils of the leaves; petals claw-like. 1-2'.
First found_____Where_____

21. FIREWEED, Epilobium angustifolium, is known the world over as a rank, tall-growing perennial which springs Brush Grass from underground root-stocks.   The panicles of densely Str. Wd. hung, rosy flowers are beautiful until the cottony seeds begin to form; leaves net-like veined beneath. 1 1/2-6' tall.
First found_____Where_____

22. CALIFORNIA FUCHSIA, Zauschneria californica, brings forth its glorious scarlet trumpets to relieve the Rocks monotony of our yellowing hillsides in late summer and Brush Str. Wd. early fall. Look for it clinging to the steepest, driest canyon walls. The base is usually slightly woody and the herbage is covered by very soft, tiny, green to gray spreading hairs; leaves linear to lanceolate. Plant 1-3' high.
First found_____Where_____

23. FAREWELL-TO-SPRING, Clarkia (Godetia) amoena, will be seen in colonies of pink splashed with crimson on the drying roadsides and low hills. It is particularly brilliant on the very cliff edges above the ocean. 5-20" tall.
First found_____Where_____

19. Fringed Clarkia
(Photo by Lula Barnes)

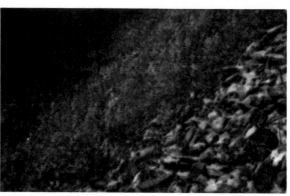

21. Fireweed
(Photo by Dennis Anderson)

20. Red Ribbons (on bank)
(Also called Lovely Clarki
(Photo by Frank Kemp)

22a. California Fuchsia
(Photo by Violet Wooden)

22b. California Fuchsia
(Photo by James McNamee)

23. Farewell to Spring
(Photo by Louise Hallberg)

5a. Indian Warriors
Photo by Lula Barnes)

24. Chinese Houses
(Photo by E. F. Jewett)

25b. Indian Warriors
(Photo by E. F. Jewett)

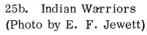

FIGWORT FAMILY   SCROPHULARIACEAE

Brush
Grass
Oak
Str. Wd.
Sav.

24. CHINESE HOUSES, Collinsia heterophylla, may be seen sheltered under bushes that line road banks. The combination of colors in the flowers may differ, but all are pretty and the symmetrical flower whorls do appear something like the pagodas of China. In this species the upper lip of the corolla is distinctly paler than the lower lip. Very common in shaded places. 8-20" high.

First found_____Where_____

Oak
Brush
Conif.

25. INDIAN WARRIOR, Pedicularis densiflora. Sometimes out in the open, but more often in light shade, whole companies of Indian Warriors stand constantly at attention with their feet firmly planted in a cluster of fern-like, pale green or bronze leaves. In one of the pictures they are guarding newly opened Easter Lilies or Fawn Lilies or Lambtongues on a beautiful bank that is no more, as it was destroyed by a new road. Of course we do need safer mountain roads, but we need lovely wildflowers too! 4-16" tall.

First found_____Where_____

26. INDIAN PAINTBRUSH, Castilleja wightii, 26b, may be discerned by its yellow to reddish-orange flowers, with all hues in between. What appear to be splashy, colorful flowers, are really glorified bracts. This species appears as far north as the southern Mendocino coastal bluffs. At the north end of its range it appears with brighter red bracts and corollas and is called C. wightii, subspecies rubra, 26a. The common darker red paintbrush inhabiting the same bluff locations from about the Sea Ranch north is called the Mendocino Coast Indian Paintbrush, C. mendocinensis (or may be a subspecies of C. latifolia), and is not pictured here but looks superficially the same as C. wightii except for the rich red color. Several other inland paintbrushes are also found in our area. 8-15" tall.

First found_____Where_____

Str. Wd.
Oak
Grass
Sav.
Brush

27. SCARLET MONKEY FLOWER, Mimulus cardinalis. The glorious Scarlet Mimulus, as it is also called, is a vivid picture when seen in blossom against the clay or rocky

banks where it is usually found, often with its feet in water.
The soft, usually sticky foliage, is light green, the flowers
crimson velvet. The pedicel or stem that holds the flower
is longer than the calyx in this species and the stamens stick
out above the corolla. 10-30" high.
First found_____Where_____

28. PURPLE MOUSE-EARS, Mimulus douglasii, form
masses of low-growing purplish flowers with prominent yellow anthers.   The common name results from the flower
having only two prominent corolla lobes.   Plant 1-3" tall.
Kellogg's Monkey Flower, M. kelloggii, is on the left of the
picture with all lobes fully developed and color rose-purple.
Both are found in places which are damp in the spring.
They are well distributed inland in rocky places. 1-8" tall.
First found_____Where_____

29. YELLOW MONKEY FLOWER, Mimulus guttatus (or
Common Monkey Flower). A sharp look at the photo on page
23 easily explains the common name. The more tender varieties come out in early spring; watch for them in the wet
places all summer. The corolla is usually spotted with red,
and its throat almost enclosed with hairy ridges. 1 1/2-36".
First found_____Where_____

Str. Wd.
Grass
Water
Oak
Brush

ORANGE BUSH MONKEY FLOWER, Mimulus auranti-
acus, varies from orange to yellow in the flowers,   and   is
common along the coast, flowering much of the year. 2-5'.
First found_____Where_____

Conif.
Rocks
Str. Wd.
Conif.
Oak
Brush

30. REDWOOD PENSTEMON, Penstemon corymbosus
(lately called Keckiella corymbosa).   These plants like to
show brick-red glory from roadside banks above and below
your eye-level, so watch closely as you criss-cross the inland Redwood Empire. Highway U.S. 101 north and south of
Richardson Grove is a favorite finding place of ours.   The
plants seem to scramble over the steep roadside embank-
ments. The stems are woody and the plants are up to 20"
high. The upper corolla lip flares at a right angle while the
lower lip spreads. It flowers profusely from August through
October. The only common woody penstemon of this area.
First found_____Where_____

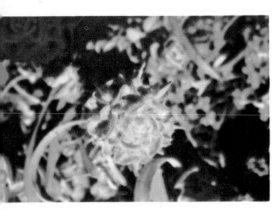

26b. Indian Paintbrush
(Photo by E. F. Jewett)

26a. Indian Paintbru
(Photo by E. F. Jewet

27. Scarlet Monkeyflower
(Photo by Violet Wooden)

28. Purple Mouse-ears and
Kellogg's Monkey Flower (le
(Photo by E. F. Jewett)

Yellow Monkeyflower
(Photo by Lula Barnes)

30. Redwood Penstemon
(Photo by Walter Knight)

32. Yellow Sand Verbena
(Photo by Frank Kemp)

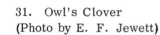

31. Owl's Clover
(Photo by E. F. Jewett)

Pink Sand Verbena (Photo by Alice Ackley)

31. OWL'S CLOVER, Orthocarpus densiflorus, comes in several different color combinations, with white and purple and yellow predominant, and the bracts purple-tipped.

Grass
Sav.
Oak

All the flowers are compacted closely on the stem, all showing rows of quaint little owl faces (plainly visible in the photograph). The upper lip of the two-lipped flower is usually straight and covered with fine hairs. The plants sometimes form masses of color in the fields. 4-14" high.

First found_____Where_____

Brush
Oak
Str. Wd.
Grass

COMMON OWL'S CLOVER, Orthocarpus purpurascens, differs in having finely-divided leaves, while the upper helmet-like lip to the corolla is hooked and bearded. 4-12".

First found_____Where_____

FOUR O'CLOCK FAMILY   NYCTAGINACEAE

Beach

32. YELLOW SAND VERBENA, Abronia latifolia. The yellow flowers and very wide leaves of this plant, as it spreads in little mats on the beach, are quite distinctive. Like other sand verbenas, it has a quite deep and spreading root system to hold the plant when it is attacked by the fierce ocean winds. The prostrate stems are from 10 to 33 inches long and densely-hairy-glandular (sticky).

First found_____Where_____

Beach

33. PINK SAND VERBENA or BEACH SAND VERBENA, Abronia umbellata, is pink most of the time, but sometimes white; the stems are often reddish and sometimes sticky to the touch; the leaves are more oval and not so wide as the above plant, and, like most Abronias, rather fleshy in texture. The extraordinary ability of these beach verbenas to adapt both to shifting sand and a heavy salt content in the atmosphere and sand shows a most interesting specialization in living that these plants portray. 8-30" long stems.

First found_____Where_____

FUMITORY FAMILY   FUMARIACEAE

Conif.
Oak
Hardw.

34. BLEEDING HEART, Dicentra formosa, ordinarily colonizes in damp, shady spots where the lovely pink to

reddish hearts hang from the curving stem like bangles on a necklace.   The cut-leaf, pale green, and fernlike foliage serves as a perfect foil for these precious woodland jewels. The leafless stems rise from a cluster of long, basal leaves to support the flowers in a compact panicle.   8-20" high.
First found_____Where_____

GENTIAN FAMILY   GENTIANACEAE

35. BLUE GENTIAN, Gentiana oregana, is rightly fabled in story and song.   The deep blue of the sky and the pale blue of distant water in the early morning are caught in the gentian's bell or bottle-shaped blooms.   Gentians are of different shapes, some tall and slender, others low-growing and sprawly, but always beautiful, with the showy flowers ranging from blue, through purple to white and even all yellow.   There are just two common ones in our area, this Blue or Oregon Gentian, which has rather broad oval leaves, and the King's or Scepter Gentian (Gentiana sceptrum), which has narrower, lanceolate leaves. Both have blue flowers, but the oregana petals are green-dotted. 8-20" tall.
First found_____Where_____

Grass Brush Meadow

HEATH FAMILY   ERICACEAE

It would take several large books to do justice to the remarkable Heath Family.   There is even confusion in the botanical world over the many different types of small flowering growths, bushes, and trees, all commonly known as heaths. Following the method of A CALIFORNIA FLORA, by Drs. Philip A. Munz and David D. Keck, we are placing our pyrolas, chimaphilas, sugarsticks, and a collection of unusually rare botanical specimens (often called heaths) in the WINTERGREEN FAMILY at the end of this book.

36. MADRONE, Arbutus menziesii, is one of the most unusual trees of the forest, with bright reddish-brown and smooth young bark changing with age into a shreddy dark-brown bark.   The pale white, urn-shaped corollas show the close relationship to the manzanitas (37 and 38). 15-125'.
First found_____Where_____

Oak Hardw.

34. Bleeding Heart
(Photo by Violet Wooden)

37a. Bearberry (jewels)
(Photo by E. F. Jewett)

36. Madrone
(Photo by E. F. Jewett)

35. Blue Gentian
(Photo by E. F. Jewett)

7b. Bearberry (berries)
Photo by Violet Wooden)

38. Common Manzanita
(Photo by James McNamee)

a. Huckleberries (flowers)
Photo by Charles Young)

39b. Huckleberries (berries)
(Photo by Charles Young)

37. BEARBERRY, <u>Arctostaphylos</u> <u>uva-ursi,</u> also called
Kinnikinnick or Sandberry, is a low, prostrate shrub that

Brush
Grass
Beach

throws up occasional erect branches, 2-6 inches tall. It
has a darker-brown and less reddish bark than most of the
manzanitas. The shining, leathery and oval leaves surround
dense clusters of whitish or pinkish, urn-shaped flowers.
Indians used the leaves for smoking and as a tonic in tea.
First found_____Where_____

Brush
Oak
Conif.

38. COMMON MANZANITA, <u>Arctostaphylos</u> <u>manzanita,</u>
also called Parry Manzanita. These erect shrubs are noted,
along with related species, for their dark red and smooth
(sometimes even glistening) bark. This species is noted for
the combination of bright green leaves with hoary-white or
grayish, hairy branchlets. The white or pink, urn-shaped
flowers turn into first white, then dark red berries. 6-21'.
It is common on dry slopes, mainly in the interior.
First found_____Where_____

39. CALIFORNIA HUCKLEBERRY, <u>Vaccinium</u> <u>ovatum,</u>
has shining, leathery green leaves with toothed edges and

Conif.
Hardw.

Brush

pale undersides; the white to pink, bell-shaped   flowers
are surrounded at first by red bracts, which fall off as the
flowers turn into black edible berries. Often these many
branched shrubs thickly cover the forest floor. This plant
reminds us of Huckleberry pie and Huckleberry Finn, and
other symbols of free wilderness life. 3-8' tall.
First found_____Where_____

40. CALIFORNIA RHODODENDRON,   <u>Rhododendron</u>
<u>macrophyllum</u>, is also called California Rose-bay, and is

Conif.
Str. Wd.
Brush

one of our most stately and beautiful woodland shrubs.   The
dark green and leathery leaves are paler below; the spectacular, bell-shaped flowers are usually rose to rose-purple in
color, rarely white, and appear in terminal umbels and racemes. 3-13' tall.
First found_____Where_____

Conif.
Brush
Str. Wd.

41. WESTERN AZALEA, <u>Rhododendron</u> <u>occidentale,</u> is
a loosely-branched shrub with deciduous leaves and shredding bark.   The leaves are much thinner and lighter green
than in the California Rhododendron.   The white to creamy

or pink flowers are funnel-shaped and very beautiful, but not quite as spectacular as its relative; they appear in terminal clusters among the large, lance-shaped leaves; the upper lobe of each corolla often has a yellowish blotch. Probably no bushes in the forest, with the possible exception of the dogwood, attract so much attention in late spring as the azaleas and rhododendrons, whose large flowers often catch the few rays of sunlight like glowing cups and fill the woods with laughter after the darkness of winter. 3-15' tall.
First found_____Where_____

42. SALAL, <u>Gaultheria shallon,</u> is usually a low and spreading shrub or sub-shrub, though sometimes tall and erect.   The ovate or round leaves are sharp-pointed and finely-toothed, usually evergreen, and are leathery to the touch.   The white or pink, urn-shaped flowers appear in racemes and turn into dark purple berries with brown seeds. It is a typical shrub of damp woodlands. 1-2 1/2' tall.
First found_____Where_____

Conif.
Str. Wd.
Brush

43. LABRADOR TEA, <u>Ledum glandulosum</u>, has shiny, leathery leaves, finely-wrinkled above, and stiff, whitish-green twigs, often somewhat sticky to the touch, and giving off a fragrant odor; the white flowers appear in dense, terminal, umbel-shaped corymbs, starting as large and scaly buds. The flowers turn into round or oblong capsules. This plant is famous as a wilderness substitute for tea and is indeed believed delicious by many who drink it. 2-6' tall.
First found_____Where_____

Water
Marsh

HONEYSUCKLE FAMILY   CAPRIFOLIACEAE

44. HAIRY HONEYSUCKLE, <u>Lonicera hispidula</u>, with its opposite leaves, which are very closely set, climbs through bushes and trees, festooning them with dainty, sweet-smelling pink clusters during the summer.   In fall and winter the flowers turn to sparkling rubies   (fruits) that are not edible.   The flowers form axillary whorls of spikes or loose panicles. 6-20' long or tall.
First found_____Where_____

Conif.
Oak
Hardw.

40. California Rhododendron
(Photo by Frank Kemp)

41. Western Azalea
(Photo by E. F. Jewett)

42. Salal
(Photo by Frank Kemp)

43. Labrador Tea
(Photo by Violet Wooden)

44. Hairy Honeysuckle
(Photo by Violet Wooden)

45. Twinberry
(Photo by E. F. Jewett)

Str. Wd.   45. TWINBERRY, <u>Lonicera involucrata,</u> is a non-twining
Oak   shrub with its opposite leaves darker green above and paler
Conif.   and more hairy below.   The flower stems usually   turn
reddish to purplish, each leading to two delicately perfect
twin flowers, the pair held attractively in a cup-like set of
bracts, and each corolla like a perfect little narrow bell.
The twinberries or fruits are black and not edible. 2-10'.
First found_____Where_____

IRIS FAMILY   IRIDACEAE

Grass   46. WILD BLUE IRIS, <u>Iris douglasiana,</u> also called
Str. Wd.   Coast Blue Iris or Douglas Iris, is the most constant bloom-
Oak   er among our several kinds. Like many other Iris flowers,
Conif.   it seems to change color in a new locality.   This species
often sends out its first blossoms in late November.   By
February, in an open winter, the roads along the coast and
the adjacent pastures are handsomely blue-dotted with them.
This species has very long leaves, up to 36" long,   dark
green to yellowish-green and with reddish or pinkish bases;
the large flowers vary in color from deep   red-purple,
through dark lavender and blue to pale cream. 10-20" tall.
First found_____Where_____

Conif.   Another common local species of this genus is PURDY'S
Oak   IRIS, <u>Iris purdyi</u> (which could be called Yellow Iris), which
Hardw.   is smaller and has cream-yellow flowers, usually veined
with purplish-brown or lavender and often lavender-tinged.
First found_____Where_____

Grass   47. BLUE-EYED GRASS or GRASS IRIS, <u>Sisyrinchium</u>
Brush   <u>bellum.</u>   This is the commonest of our Iris plants, filling
Str. Wd.   many a meadow or grassland with its clusters of long, very
Oak   slender and knife-like leaves from which the blue, violet,
Conif.   lilac or sometimes white flowers emerge in the springtime.
The flowers turn into pale or dark brown capsules, filled
with one to a few dark-pitted seeds. Its great numbers and
ability to live in many different habitats show its wonder-
ful adaptability to different environments. 4-20" tall.
First found_____Where_____

GOLDEN-EYED GRASS (<u>S. californicum</u>); yellow flowers.
First found_____Where_____

LILY FAMILY   LILIACEAE

This enormous family has some of the most beautiful and unique flowers in all our area. First to be mentioned of these are the Wild Onions, of which about five species are found in the Redwood Empire. The three most commonly seen and wide-spread of these are mentioned below.

48. ONE-LEAVED WILD ONION, Allium unifolium. In our particular part of the Mendocino County coast there are many swamps that are the favorite dwelling place of **this** beautifully-shaped, waxy-pink wild onion. There are many flowers in a loose umbel, a few of them appearing lilac or even white, each with yellow or purplish stamens nestled in the heart of the flower. 8-25" tall.

Marsh
Grass

First found_____Where_____

49. MAGENTA WILD ONION or COASTAL WILD ONION, Allium dichlamydeum, frequents the edges of marshy areas in the open meadows. We have also found this bright magenta beauty growing in steep and rocky places. It looks for all the world like our cultivated amaryllis, or naked ladies, since the foliage is gone before the blossoms appear. The rank onion smell is most evident. The flowers form very congested umbels and their rich rose-purple color (magenta) is distinctive. Most wild onions are edible, at least at certain times of the year, but some are very bitter. 4-12" tall.

Rock
Brush
Conif.
Grass

First found_____Where_____

SCYTHE-LEAVED WILD ONION, Allium falcifolium, is characterized by sickle-shaped leaves, and deep rose to purple flowers or sometimes greenish-white, tinged with rose. 6-12" high.

Rocks
Conif.
Brush

First found_____Where_____

50. TALL BRODIAEA or BLUE DICKS or WILD HYACINTH, Brodiaea laxa, is one of the several lovely Brodiaea species found in our valleys and hills. The blue or violet (rarely white) flowers are surrounded by purple bracts. The bulb is edible; leaves flat and keeled. 6-16".

Grass
Str. Wd.
Oak

First found_____Where_____

34

47. Blue-eyed Grass
(Photo by Charles Young)

46. Wild Blue Iris
(Photo by Lula Barnes)

48. One-leaved Wild Onion
(Photo by Lula Barnes)

49. Magenta Wild Onion
(Photo by Charles Young)

50. Tall Brodiaea
(Photo by Violet Wooden)

51. Dwarf Brodiaea
(Photo by Lula Barnes)

52. Blue Stars
(Photo by E. F. Jewett)

51.   DWARF BRODIAEA, <u>Brodiaea</u> <u>coronaria</u> <u>macropoda</u> (or <u>terrestris</u>). This very low-growing form is particularly common in the meadows near woods. The flowers are lilac to violet.   Up to 3" tall.   This is a dwarf form of the Harvest Brodiaea (<u>B</u>. <u>coronaria</u>), which forms its flowers in a comparatively flat-topped umbel and is more common in the Great Valley.   4-15" tall.

Conif.
Oak
Grass

First seen_____Where_____

52.   BLUE STARS or STAR-FLOWERED BRODIAEA, <u>Brodiaea</u> <u>stellaris.</u>   The perianth (sepals and petals) of this medium-sized Brodiaea flatten out rather abruptly in a way unusual in this genus to produce a star-like appearance, so that a number of them in a meadow appear very much like a group of scattered violet-purple stars with white centers. The bottoms of the perianth tubes are greenish. 4-12" tall.

Grass
Meadow
Conif.

First seen_____Where_____

53.   CHINESE FIRECRACKERS, FIRECRACKER FLOWER, or FIRECRACKER LILY, <u>Brodiaea</u> <u>ida-maia</u>, is, perhaps, our most distinctive native lily.   It may be found dangling several bright red firecrackers, each scalloped with green, on grassy hillsides bordering our   mountain roads at elevations from 1000 to 4000 feet.   It flowers in May to July.   1-3' tall.

Grass
Meadow
Conif.

First seen_____Where_____

54.   REDWOOD LILY, <u>Lilium</u> <u>rubescens.</u>   This is the first of the magnificent tall lilies mentioned in this book, and, like the others, it has several common names (including Lilac Lily). Beauty is the attribute all have in common, and all grow in the Redwood Empire, but, like gold, they are where you find them! The 3-8 white flowers are purple-spotted, later turning wine-colored. Because it is the most common large lily found in the chaparral or brush, it is often called Chaparral Lily or even Chamise Lily, after a particular plant (Chamise) with which it is associated. 2-8' tall. A lovely flower of heavenly fragrance, it should be left alone.

Brush
Conif.

First seen_____Where_____

55. TIGER LILY, LEOPARD LILY or PANTHER LILY, Lilium pardalinum, has been called Tiger Lily so long that it is hard to take the name away from it, though Leopard Lily is a much more appropriate name because it is definitely spotted instead of striped. The flowers are rarely fragrant, as in the Redwood Lily, but, as they nod in the breeze (forming 1 to several on each plant), their orange (or red) color, spotted with maroon, makes them one of the most attractive sights in the woods. 3-7 1/2' tall.
Str. Wd. Grass Meadow Rocks

First found_____Where_____

56. KELLOGG'S LILY, Lilium kelloggii, is found in dryer places than the Leopard Lily. Its fragrant flowers are large and distinctively pink or pale pink in color, with a central yellow band that is sometimes dotted with purple; the whole flower may turn rose-purple with aging; there are 1-15 or even more flowers on each plant, all with their outer edges rolled back. 2-10' tall.
Conif. Rocks

First found_____Where_____

57. COAST LILY, Lilium maritimum, strangely enough grows in masses on the edges of coastal openings and, at such places, appears actually in miniature. Normally it is 1-5' tall, with 1-12 horizontal and bell-shaped flowers, each dark red and spotted with maroon. It particularly likes raised hummocks in bogs, but also sandy soil. Botanists are constantly referring to the white plains of Mendocino and THE PYGMY FOREST there is well-known for its tiny but full-grown plants, bushes, and trees. Nature plays us flower lovers tricks sometimes, but it is good teaching!
Marsh Sand Oak Brush

58. EUREKA LILY, Lilium occidentale, or WESTERN LILY, is particularly common near Eureka. It is found most often near the ocean and is distinguished by being usually dark red flowered or dark orange, with maroon spots; later it may fade to purple, but always has a green center in each flower. The flowers have the outer half recurving under. It likes wet places and is especially associated with ferns. 2-12' tall.
Brush Sand

First found_____Where_____

38

53. Chinese Firecrackers
(Photo by Donal McCall)

54. Redwood Lily
(Photo by Violet Wooden)

55. Tiger Lilies
(Photo by Violet Wooden)

56. Kellogg's Lily 39
(Photo by Paul Bowman)

57. Coast Lily
(Photo by Violet Wooden)

58. Eureka Lily
(Photo by Paul Bowman)

59. Bolander's Lily
(Photo by Violet Wooden)

60. Mission Bells
(Photo by Dennis Anderson)

59. BOLANDER'S LILY, Lilium bolanderi, is another
Brush
Conif.
very beautiful big lily with flowers varying from pale scarlet to deep crimson, each speckled with purple spots; only
the upper margins of such flowers are rolled back;
1-4" tall.
First found_____Where_____

The extraordinarily lovely COLUMBIA or OREGON LILY,
Lilium columbianum, is found only in the northern part of
our region. It has orange-yellow or lemon yellow flowers,
though sometimes deep scarlet with a yellow center, and
generally spotted with maroon. Dry places. 2-6' tall.
First found_____Where_____

60. MISSION BELLS, or CHECKER LILY, Fritillaria
lanceolata, is extraordinarily varied in shape, color, and
growth. Usually it is more somber in appearance than the
big lilies just mentioned, but it's softer colors are often
very spiritual and lovely in effect, particularly this species,
whose delicate, hanging-bell-like flowers are mottled with
yellow against purple-brown, or may vary to pale greenish-
yellow, faintly mottled with purple, each appearing like a
deep, upside-down bowl. Often found elf-like in shade. 1-4'.
First found_____Where_____

61a. MENDOCINO MISSION BELLS, Fritillaria roder-
icki. Found in scattered areas on the Mendocino coast and
inland in Anderson Valley. Distinctive for the beige thumb-
nail delicately marked on each brown petal point. 8-10" tall.
First found_____Where_____

61b. SCARLET FRITILLARY, Fritillaria recurva, lives
on dry hillsides in brush. The 1-9 nodding flowers are com-
Brush
Conif.
bined funnel and bell-shaped, bright scarlet, checkered with
yellow within and tinged purple on the outside. There is a
prominent oval, yellow gland with red spots. 1-3' tall.
First found_____Where_____

PURDY'S FRITILLARY, Fritillaria purdyi, looks some-
Brush
Conif.
thing like Mission Bells, but has white flowers, mottled with
purple lines and spots. 8-16" tall.
First found_____Where_____

ADOBE LILY, Fritillaria pluriflora, is rather fantastic
looking, with 1-3 nodding, bell-shaped, pink to pink-purple
flowers, generally with brown veins outside. 8-20" tall.
Oak
First found_____Where_____

The Mariposa Lilies of the genus Calochortus are a particularly distinctive and beautiful group of flowers of our woods, each with delicate, fairy-like colors.

62. HAIRY CAT'S EAR, HAIRY STAR TULIP or PUSSY EARS, Calochortus tolmiei (or maweanus), may be found in grassy meadows and along roadbanks. The ears may be grayish-lavender or yellow, but cat's ears they are, unmistakably. There is a very narrow, basal leaf, 4-16 inches long. The white or cream flowers are sometimes tinged with rose or purple, each petal having a beard on its inner face (as do most Mariposa Lilies). 4-16" tall. _Conif. Oak Hardw._
First found_____Where_____

63. BABY TULIP or LARGE-FLOWERED STAR TULIP, Calochortus uniflorus, looks very much like a baby tulip, but is noted also for its satiny flowers and the peculiar greenish-lilac sepals. The petals are generally lilac with a purple spot on each side of the gland, and much less hairy than the above flower. 4-10" tall. _Grass Meadow_
First found_____Where_____

64. BUTTERFLY MARIPOSA LILY, Calochortus venustus. While the Spanish word Mariposa means butterfly, the Latin word Calochortus means beautiful grass. So the botanists chose very beautiful and appropriate names for the flowers of this genus. This particular flower is no more butterfly-like than any of the others, except that it may be called so because it shows so many different colors, with a brown spot surrounded by yellow on each sepal, while the petals are white or lilac with a prominent dark eye-spot in the middle and a reddish blotch near the top. 4-32" tall. _Grass Meadow_
First found_____Where_____

YELLOW MARIPOSA LILY, Calochortus luteus, is noted for its wonderful deep yellow color, either streaked or spotted with brown on the petals. 6-20" tall. _Grass Meadow_
First found_____Where_____

65. DIOGENES LANTERN or GOLDEN FAIRY LANTERN, Calochortus amabilis (also called Yellow Globe-Tulip and Golden Fairybells), brightens our hilly roadsides with _Oak Grass Conif._

61b. Scarlet Fritillary
(Photo by Violet Wooden)

61a. Mendocino Mission Bells
(Photo by Charles Young)
Honors Wayne Roderick

62a. Cat's Ears (close
(Hairy Star Tulip)
(Photo by Violet Wooden

62b. Cat's Ears
(Photo by Violet Wooden)

3. Baby Tulips
Photo by E. F. Jewett)

64. Butterfly Mariposa Lily
(Photo by E. F. Jewett)

5. Diogenes Lantern
Photo by Violet Wooden)

66. Slink Pod
(Photo by Alice Ackley)

waxy, golden yellow lanterns set off by bluish-green foliage. The stout stems fork in pairs. 8-12" tall.
First found_____Where_____

Conif.
Oak
Hardw.
 A similar looking species is the WHITE FAIRY LANTERN, <u>Calochortus</u> <u>albus</u>. The sepals are greenish-white, often touched with purple; the white petals are purplish at the base and with a patch of yellowish hair. 8-20" tall.
First found_____Where_____

Conif.
 66. SLINK POD, <u>Scoliopus</u> <u>bigelovii</u>, also answers to the names of Fetid Adder's Tongue or Brownies. The names are suggestive indeed; the Greek derivation means "crooked foot" because of the twisted pedicels or stems. The mottled green and purple flowers have a bad odor. It is sometimes found as early as December 15 in the damp Mendocino County coastal area known as "the Banana Belt. " They literally spring from the ground in their haste to be the "first lily" to bloom. Dark mottled leaves are also distinctive. 4-8" tall.
First found_____Where_____

Meadow
Water
Conif.
Str. Wd.
 67. PINK FAWN LILY, <u>Erythronium</u> <u>revolutum</u>, which we have found on Redwood Creek near Willow Creek (Highway 299), and in the Siskiyous on the way to Grants Pass, is rather rare, but surely lovely. The 1-4 buds may start out creamy white, with yellow at the base, but soon turn rose-pink in color. Also called Coast Fawn Lily. 4-12" tall.
First found_____Where_____

Brush
Conif
 68. CREAM FAWN LILY, <u>Erythronium</u> <u>californicum</u>, is also called Lambstongue, Easter Lily and Trout Lily, all on account of the spotted and mottled leaves. The usually reddish flower stems support 1 to 3 or more white to cream colored flowers with greenish-yellow bases and cross bands of yellow, orange or brown. Very common. 4-10" tall.
First found_____Where_____

Conif.
 The OREGON FAWN LILY, <u>Erythronium</u> <u>oregonum</u>, ssp. <u>leucandrum</u>, is similar to the above flowers, but the white or pink flowers have reddish or brown bases outside, and yellow within, and their tips are twisted. The flower stems are brownish and about 6 to 12 inches tall.
First found_____Where_____

69. BEAR GRASS, Xerophyllum tenax, also known as Elk Grass, Fire Lily, Pine Lily, or Squaw Grass, is truly spectacular in beauty as well as in historical lore. The wiry tufts of stiff grass from which the tall shafts of bloom arise are grayish-green and very strong. Therefore, they were used by the Indians in the making of baskets and rope, also for the same things by the early pioneers who were glad to find these plants growing by their cabins. They are often seen in mountain meadows and frequently grow in banks along Highway 1. The numerous white flowers appear in a dense, terminal raceme, 4-24" long. 1-6' tall.
First found_____Where_____

Grass
Conif.

70. WAKE ROBIN, Trillium ovatum. Since the Wake Robins have already done their duty this spring of 1964, and the zygadene lilies are almost a foot high right now in Grandpa Charley's Park, let's take a moment to tell how these and other lovely wild flowers MAY get under your skin, too. For the first year or two we were in this gorgeous natural spot near Gualala Chas would calmly report new findings rather prosaically, but one sunny morning in early January he called, "Hurry out! Trillies are poking through, and zyggies are up all over the place!"
Our Wake Robin, or Coast Trillium has its own little stem, which holds the flower way up above the three large leaves; white flowers turn rose color. 8-20" tall.
First found_____Where_____

Conif.

71. RED TRILLIUM or GIANT WAKE ROBIN, Trillium chloropetalum, has its red (also white, see below) blossoms nestling right among the three large leaves, and, therefore is sessile, or without the little stem. 12-20" tall.
First found_____Where_____

Conif.
Oak
Str. Wd.
Brush

72. WHITE TRILLIUM, Trillium chloropetalum. Same species as above, but shown in picture is the white variety. Both grow in the damp woods, flowering from early February and on, throughout most of the Redwood Empire. 12-20".
First found_____Where_____

67. Pink Fawn Lily
(Photo by Lula Barnes)

68. Cream Fawn Lily
(Photo by Violet Wooden)

69. Bear Grass
(Photo by Violet Wooden)

70. Wake Robin
(Photo by Gordon McBride)

71. Red Trillium
(Photo by Louise Hallberg)

4. Zygadene Lily
Photo by E. F. Jewett)

72. White Trillium
(Photc by Lula Barnes)

73. Creek Trillium
(Photo by Violet Wooden)

73.   CREEK TRILLIUM, <u>Trillium</u> <u>rivale,</u> is rather rare and unusual, but may be found along streams with rocky, canyon-like walls.   The smaller leaves and longer flower stem give it a more vine-like appearance   than its   bigger cousins.   The white petals may be marked with rose-red. 4-11" tall.

Str. Wd.
Rocks
Conif.

First found_____Where_____

74.   ZYGADENE LILY or STAR LILY, <u>Zygadenus</u> <u>fre-</u> <u>montii,</u> is among a genus that has more or less poisonous bulbs.   The yellowish-white flowers of this species   have clawed petals and appear in rather loose panicles or ra-cemes.   The 8-24" basal leaves are folded and arched.

Grass
Brush
Conif.

First found_____Where_____

DEATH CAMAS, <u>Zygadenus</u> <u>venenosus,</u> is noted for its very poisonous bulb, which has a dark outer coat. The bas-al leaves are 6-12" long and folded, but not arched.   The white flowers have both sepals and petals long-clawed. 10-24" tall.

Grass
Brush
Conif.
Meadow
Str. Wd.

First found_____Where_____

SMALL-FLOWERED ZYGADENE, <u>Zygadenus</u> <u>micranthus</u> has flowers only about 1/4" long. 8-20" tall plant. Raceme.

Brush
Conif.

First found_____Where_____

LARGE-PANICLED ZYGADENE,   <u>Zygadenus</u> <u>fontanus.</u> The large panicles have widely-spreading,   horizontal branches; basal leaves folded and rough to touch. 1-3' tall.

Conif.
Brush

First found_____Where_____

75.   CORN LILY, <u>Veratrum</u> <u>fimbriatum,</u> is also called False Hellebore.   Very stout with long leaves that hug the stock like corn.   Grows in great colonies in our Mendocino woodland areas in light or deep shade or even sun.   It is a late summer bloomer with blossoms still lovely well into winter. 3-7' tall.

Conif.
Meadow

First found_____Where_____

76. RED CLINTONIA, <u>Clintonia</u> <u>andrewsiana</u>, is a fa-vorite lily of the damp woodsy mixed redwood forest.   The very long flower stem has a rosette of large, shiny, bright green leaves clustered at its feet; the reddish flowers form

Conif.

an umbel, which crowns the tall, sturdy stem. Sometimes smaller clusters are found below the main one. The berries are bright blue "jewels." Plant 1-2' tall.
First found_____Where_____

77. FALSE SOLOMON'S SEAL, <u>Smilacina</u> amplexicaulis, Conif. is often found with Fairy Bells (see below) waving its plumes Str. Wd. or bells along some shady bank. This species has numerous white flowers on a large, 1 1/2-7" long panicle; the broad, but sharp-pointed leaves clasp the stem near the base. 1-3' tall, with mostly red or purple-spotted berries.
First found_____Where_____

NUTTALL'S SOLOMON SEAL, <u>Smilacina</u> <u>stellata</u> var. <u>sessilifolia</u>, has a few or several white flowers in a short Conif. raceme; leaves with 3 prominent veins; berries red. 1-2'. Brush Str. Wd.
First found_____Where_____

78. FAIRY BELLS, <u>Disporum</u> <u>smithii</u>, certainly deserves its name, as the delicate pale greenish-white flowers are hidden under the large, oval but sharp-pointed leaves Conif. exactly as one might suspect a fairy would do with her bells, Str. Wd. which the flowers indeed look like. This species has unusually large flowers, 5/8-1" long, so is sometimes called Large-Flowered Fairy Bells, and has light-orange to red berries, looking like delicate jewels. 1-3' tall.
First found_____Where_____

HOOKER'S FAIRY BELL, <u>Disporum</u> <u>hookeri</u>, has a cluster of 1-3 top-shaped flowers, creamy-white to greenish- Conif. white in color, turning into bright scarlet berries. 1-2 1/2'. Str. Wd.
First found_____Where_____

LOASA FAMILY   LOASACEAE

79. BLAZING STAR, <u>Mentzelia</u> <u>laevicaulis</u>, often grows on gravel bars on dry creeks, where the stars make a gold- Grass en glow mornings and evenings. Be careful of the branches; Brush Str. Wd. they will stick to your clothes. A flower of the hot summer. Oak The leaves become brittle and rough to the feel; the unusu- Conif. ally large, 2-3" long, light yellow flowers form clusters of Hardw. 1-3 at the top of the shining white stem. Plant 1-5' tall.
First found_____Where_____

50

76a. Clintonia
(Photo by Frank Kemp)

75. Corn Lily
(Photo by Louise Hallberg)

76b. Clintonia
(Photo by Alice Ackley)

77. False Solomon's Seal
(Photo by Frank Kemp)

Blazing Stars
oto by Lula Barnes)

80. Wild Hollyhock
(Photo by E. F. Jewett)

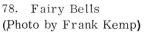

82. Milkwort
(Photo by E. F. Jewett)

81. Meadow Foam
(Photo by Violet Wooden)

MALLOW FAMILY   MALVACEAE

Grass
Brush

80. WILD HOLLYHOCK or CHECKERBLOOM, Sidalcea malvaeflora, is one of the taller, bushier mallows, which is found late in the season flowering along our cross-country roads. Its lower stem is covered with coarse hairs; the broad, well-rounded leaves are 3/4-2" wide and rather fleshy as well as hairy, each on a long stem, and with 7-9 lobes; the usually simple racemes are dense to open, with rose-pink to rarely white flowers, usually white-veined on the petals, which are short-beaked. 6-18" tall.
First found_____Where_____

Grass
Brush

FRINGED SIDALCEA, Sidalcea diploscypha, is one of the common pink to purple mallows of the coast, but the pink petals often have a deep purplish spot. It is a simple or few branched plant, with conspicuous finger-like bracts, often with still finer divisions or filaments, surrounding the flowers. The plant is covered with fine hairs. 8-18" tall.
First found_____Where_____

MEADOW FOAM FAMILY   LIMNANTHACEAE

Meadow
Grass
Water

81. MEADOW FOAM, Limnanthes douglasii, covers our mountain meadows with its soft and glowing yellow-white haze, charming both close by and in the distance, surely an early April delight. It is a widely-varied plant, with some petals all yellow, some white, and others yellow with white tips, each bowl-shaped and with a U-shaped band of short hairs at base of each petal. 4-16" tall.
First found_____Where_____

MILKWORT FAMILY   POLYGALACEAE

Grass
Brush

82. CALIFORNIA MILKWORT, Polygala californica, is abundant in openings and pastures in the Mendocino coast area. Here in Grandpa Charley's Park the foliage is branchy and low-growing, bronzy purple.   The blossoms, very like little sweetpeas, are rosy or pale rose, and appear in distinctly short-stemmed racemes, each with 3-10 loose flowers. Leaves have sharp, stiff hairs along veins. 1-14" tall.
First found_____Where_____

MORNING-GLORY FAMILY   CONVOLVULACEAE

83. BEACH MORNING-GLORY, <u>Convolvulus soldanella</u>, finds sandy beaches ideal for its spreading habits, since it spreads flatly over the sand to avoid the wind. The stems are fleshy; the shining leaves are almost as broad as long; the rose to purple flowers appear like short funnels, 1 1/2-2" long. It stretches out for 4 to 20" across the sand. *(Beach)*
First found_____Where_____

COMMON BINDWEED, <u>Convolvulus arvensis</u>, is a pest of our orchards and fields, twining or creeping over the ground, with single stems holding up the white to pinkish flowers, each about 1/2-2" wide at mouth. Plant 1-3' long. *(Grass Cultiv.)*
First found_____Where_____

MUSTARD FAMILY   CRUCIFERAE

(Str. Wd.)
84. SPRING BEAUTY, <u>Dentaria californica</u>, also called Toothwort or Milk-maids, often flowers in February. Colors range from white to very bright rose-purple (as pictured). It is probably our best known very early spring flower, and is surely a beauty. 4-16" tall. *(Conif. Oak Brush Grass)*
First found_____Where_____

ORCHID FAMILY   ORCHIDACEAE

85. REDWOOD ORCHID, <u>Calypso bulbosa</u>, answers also to Fairyslipper, Angel's Slipper, and Deer-head Orchid. It is one of our earliest spring flowers, and, near sea-level, a single bloom or two may be found in the first of February, so there is a long season for finding these rose-pink beauties bursting into glorious color in the mountain glades. These dainty plants show their appreciation of the first warm September rains by unfurling a single leaf out into a point to support the forthcoming bud-capped stem. Entire mossy logs may be covered by a colony of calypsos. A new weighing-in-station for a local lumber mill was about to doom a small log section covered by moss and calypsos, sturdy in spite of nearby tossed beer cans, when we rescued the flowers. Careless picking and logging destroys these beauties, but it can be stopped. Squirrels eat the bulbs. 2-10" tall. *(Conif. Str. Wd.)*
First found_____Where_____

83. Beach Morning Glory
(Photo by Frank Kemp)

85a. Redwood Orchid
(Photo by Lula Barnes)

84. Spring Beauty
(Photo by Frank Ke

86. Ladyslipper
(Photo by Dennis And

85b. White (or Giant Albine
Orchid (Photo by Charles Y

87. Chatterbox Orchid
(Photo by Lula Barnes)

88. Phantom Orchid
(Photo by Louise Hallberg)

Coral Root
hoto by E. F. Jewett)

90. Redwood Sorrel
(Photo by Lula Barnes)

Conif.
Rocks

86. CALIFORNIA LADYSLIPPER, Cypripedium califor-
nicum, clusters in shaded woods or banks of moist lime-
stone; beautiful and rare, but once seen, never to be forgot-
ten. This species has alternate leaves and 5/8" long green
yellow sepals. Petal lip white or pinkish. 1-2' tall.
First found_____Where_____

Conif.
Rocks

CLUSTERED LADYSLIPPER, Cypripedium fascicula-
tum, is smaller (2-6" tall), has opposite leaves,   and   a
greenish-yellow lip to the flower.
First found_____Where_____

Conif.
Oak
Str. Wd.
Brush

87. CHATTERBOX ORCHID, Epipactus gigantea,   or
Stream Orchis, is a stoutish plant, which lives along wet
stream banks.   The rosy blossoms are typically orchid-
like, but, unlike the rarer orchids, they may be found in
great colonies in summer. Flowers in racemes. 1-3' tall.
First found_____Where_____

Conif.

88. PHANTOM ORCHID, Eburophyton austinae (from the
Latin words meaning Ivory Plant because it is not green; often called Ghost Plant). It has a single white stem 8-10" or
more tall with waxy-white, golden-throated flowers in   a
terminal raceme. Like the calypsos, phantom orchids are
often found in colonies, but are actually quite rare.   We
came across our first one unexpectedly in early June, 1958,
as we were helping prepare our sister's Orleans ranch for
summer visitors. Grandson Mike came running in from the
forest with the exciting announcement that Grandpa Charley
had found a snow plant! It was a snow-white plant, all right.
Three tall single stems rose from the edge of a rotten log,
ending in waxy-white and plump, sort of globe-shaped flowers.   Inside we could see the shining, golden spot on the
throat, while from the plant rose a heavenly fragrance. As
Grandpa likes to tease, we forgave him for calling it a Snow
Plant. Since then we have had the pleasure of finding phan-
toms in other places near Orleans, in several shady, deeply
forested glades in southern Mendocino County,   and   inland
toward Mt. Anthony. We hope the thrill of YOUR first phantom orchid will be as lasting as ours, but please save   the
flower and teach others not to pick these rare beauties.
First found_____Where_____

89. CORAL ROOT, Corallorhiza maculata, or SPOTTED
CORAL ROOT, is the spotted species.   All Coral Roots
stand stiffly at attention as you pass through their deeply   Conif.
shaded forest home.   They stay in bloom a long time; the
blossoms are succeeded by equally interesting seed pods,
which hang down from the stems like ornaments. 8-20" tall.
First found_____Where_____

STRIPED CORAL ROOT, Corallorhiza striata, has the
flower longitudinally striped. 6-20" tall.   Conif.
First found_____Where_____

OXALIS FAMILY   OXALIDACEAE

90. REDWOOD SORREL, Oxalis oregana, is truly a
"sour" grass which carpets our redwood forests everywhere with its clover-like foliage. We transplanted some
mangled plants from a logging road and they did very well
until two of our frequent young fawn visitors decided to see
if they WERE good to eat. Apparently the deer were only   Conif.
curious since other patches in the woods are seldom disturbed by them.   The pink bloom glows brightly in   the
rounded clusters of shamrock-like leaves. 3-8" tall.
First found_____Where_____

PEA FAMILY   LEGUMINOSAE

91. REDBUD, Cercis occidentalis, is among many members of the Pea Family that contribute a great deal to our
spring and summer parade of color. Lake County is famous   Oak
for its Redbud flowers, but the plant is scattered throughout   Brush
the REDWOOD EMPIRE, and ranges from shrubs to branchy
trees, entirely clothed in springtime in sparkling, rosy magenta blossoms before the leaves unfold. 6-20' tall.
First found_____Where_____

92. CHAPARRAL PEA, Pickeringia montana, is equally
bright, but its blossoms are often hidden by the pale green   Brush
foliage and appear later in the summer. Watch out for its
spines! Branches very stiff; leaves tiny, palmately 1-3; the
large rosy flowers are solitary. 2-7' tall.
First found_____Where_____

91. Redbud
(Photo by Frank Sappingfield)

92. Chaparral Pea
(Photo by Louise Hallberg)

93. Lotus
(Photo by Lula Barnes)

94. Indian Pink
(Photo by Lula Barnes)

95.   Fringed Pink
(Photo by Alice Ackley)

96.   Yellow Pond Lily
(Photo by Frank Kemp)

97.   Cream Cups
(Photo by E. F. Jewett)

98.   Star Flower
(Photo by Frank Kemp)

Conif.
Oak
Brush
Str. Wd.
Grass

93. LARGE-FLOWERED LOTUS or PERSIAN CARPET, Lotus grandiflorus, does look like such a carpet when seen in its favorite haunt, a sunny, mountain meadow, with its many different color combinations, orange, through gold, yellow, and cream. Its purple with splashes of red dots and stripes has to be seen to be appreciated.   Imagine all this done in velvet trailers on the ground or climbing through taller grasses and you have found Lotus. It is covered with sharp and stiff, incurved and pressed down hairs. 7-9 leaflets; 2 or more yellow to red flowers in umbels. 8-24" long.
First found_____Where_____

PINK FAMILY   CARYOPHYLLACEAE

Many of our choicest pinks are pink in color, true indeed, but they are called pinks because their blossoms seem to have been cut from sparkling cloth with pinking shears.

Brush
Oak
Conif.

94. INDIAN PINK, Silene californica, makes a brilliant splash of "Indian crimson" against the greenery and rocks of our clayey roadside banks. Sticky to touch. 6-15" tall.
First found_____Where_____

Conif.
Rocks

95. FRINGED PINK, Silene hookeri, is found mainly from Humboldt Co. north, but we have seen it near Willits in Mendocino Co.   It is simply exquisite, shining away among the withered oak leaves high on a dry, rocky bank. The pink foliage is hairy, grayish, and usually spreads from a central, very deep root system prostrate on the ground; the grayish leaves often finger-like. The petals are white to pink or violet, the seeds purplish-black. 2-6" long.
First found_____Where_____

POND LILY FAMILY   NYMPHAEACEAE

Water

96. YELLOW POND LILY, or WATER LILY, Nymphaea polysepala, lives in ponds and lakes. The seeds were a common food for the Indians in the old days. Leaves either float or are erect and are deeply heart-shaped; flowers large and yellow to purplish. Plant 4 to 6' long.
First found_____Where_____

POPPY FAMILY   PAPAVERACEAE

Everybody loves the beautiful golden California Poppy, but there are other lovely members of this family too and we wish we had room for more than the one shown here.

97. CREAM CUPS, <u>Platystemon</u> <u>californicus</u>, may be Grass
seen covering entire fields in the early springtime.   Herb- Brush Meadow
age covered with soft fine hairs. 4-12" tall.
First found_____Where_____

PRIMROSE FAMILY   PRIMULACEAE

98. STAR FLOWER, <u>Trientalis</u> <u>latifolia,</u> is a slender Conif.
plant with beautifully shaped pale pink stars on delicate
stems above large, fan-shaped leaves.   It gives the im-
pression of fairy-like grace beneath the towering giants of
the redwood forest. 2-8" tall.
First found_____Where_____

99. HENDERSON'S SHOOTING STAR, <u>Dodecatheon</u> <u>hen-</u>
<u>dersonii</u>, whose brilliant magenta-purple blooms are accent-
ed by a black point in the center, are sometimes   called Oak Brush
bird-bills. Among our very earliest spring blossoms, they Str. Wd.
are also among the showiest and are to be found in clusters Grass
along roadsides protected by low brush. The petals are abruptly bent downward and backward. 3-12" tall.
First found_____Where_____

100. To find BLUE or SCARLET PIMPERNEL, <u>Anagallis</u>
<u>arvensis</u>, separately is an enjoyable experience, but now Cultiv.
imagine finding them growing side by side! Although a weed, Grass
the blossoms, with their flat and slightly attached petals Brush
(sometimes white too) are very attractive. 4-10" tall.
First found_____Where_____

PURSLANE or PORTULACA FAMILY   PORTULACACEAE

101. RED MAIDS, <u>Calandrinia</u> <u>ciliata,</u> have succulent,
wide-spreading stems, which support the many rose blooms Cultiv.
of this common roadside and meadow beauty. The racemes Grass
of 3-7, soft, rose-red flowers are lovely. 2-8" tall.
First found_____Where_____

100. Blue & Scarlet Pimpernels
(Photo by Lula Barnes)

99. Shooting Stars
(Photo by Lula Barne

101. Red Maids
(Photo by E. F. Jewett)

102a. & b. Cliff Maidens
(Photo a. by Charles Young,
photo b. by Wayne Roderick)

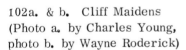

103. Wild Rose
(Photo by E. F. Jewett)

104. Sea Foam
(Photo by Frank Kemp)

105. Toyon Berry
(Photo by James McNamee)

6. Pacific Silver-weed
hoto by Louise Hallberg)

Rocks

102.   CLIFF MAIDENS, <u>Lewisia</u> <u>cotyledon,</u> is one of our very favorite wildflowers.   It grows high up on rocky cliffs from a deep tap root, topped with a cluster of thick leaves from which grow slender stems each capped with a luscious many-petaled, whitish, waxy bloom. The exquisite gleaming daintiness of the plant is further accented by the fact that each mid-rib of each petal is a pure streak of bright magenta or rosy pink.   One entire rocky bank of these fascinating flowers was blasted away on Highway 96 at Bluff Creek to provide a safer road into the Klamath River area. Summer bloomers these are, and they are worth looking for.   4-12".
First found_____Where_____

ROSE FAMILY   ROSACEAE

Wild roses are numerous, but the entire Rose Family has many seemingly unrelated members.

Oak
Brush
Conif.
Str. Wd.

103.   WILD ROSE or WOOD ROSE, <u>Rosa gymnocarpa</u>, is probably the most common of the genus. The large flowers (with 1/2" petals) are usually solitary and red in color; the branches are lined with slender, straight prickles. 3-10' .
First found_____Where_____

Conif.
Brush

104.   SEA FOAM, OCEAN SPRAY or CREAM BUSH, <u>Ho-lodiscus</u> <u>discolor</u>, has dark red to brownish or gray older bark, which shreds with age; twigs straw-colored. The tiny creamy white flowers are so numerous they well deserve the beautiful name of spray; leaves deeply-toothed. 4-20'.
First found_____Where_____

Brush
Oak

105.   TOYON or CHRISTMAS BERRY, <u>Photinia</u> <u>arbuti-folia</u>, decorates our hills in fall with bright red berries for the winter holidays.   The leathery, toothed leaves are also very Christmasy and very dark green above, but lighter below.   The many small white flowers appear in large corymbose panicles at the ends of the branches. 6-20' tall bush.
First found_____Where_____

Beach

106.   PACIFIC SILVERWEED, <u>Potentilla</u> <u>egedii,</u> var. <u>grandis,</u> is a low-growing "rose" making its home on sandy beaches, and surrounded by erect basal leaves, green above,

but often white-hairy below. The yellow petals on the flowers are about 7/16" long, flowering Apr.-Aug. 8-20" tall.
First found_____Where_____

107. SALMONBERRY, <u>Rubus spectabilis</u>,   produces Conif.
beautiful red to yellow to salmon-colored berries in the
summer that look very much like salmon eggs. The older
twigs and branches have yellowish, shredding bark; leaves
with 3 leaflets, each double-toothed; the scattered red-purple flowers appear in groups of 1-4. 6-13' tall.
First found_____Where_____

SILK-TASSEL FAMILY   GARRYACEAE

108. COAST SILK-TASSEL BUSH, <u>Garrya elliptica</u>,
hangs out its jeweled catkins ever so much like strings of
beads very early in the spring, in January, even, on the Brush
coast. The highly-polished, leather leaves give the bush a Conif.
glorious sheen, which enhances the swinging jewels. The Bluffs
hairs of the lower leaf surface in this species are usually
curly or wavy; leaves quite broad. Up to 25' tall.
First found_____Where_____

FREMONT'S SILK-TASSEL, <u>Garrya fremontii</u>, is smaller, 5-15' tall, with the lower leaf surface mostly smooth. Brush
First found_____Where_____ Conif.

SAXIFRAGE FAMILY   SAXIFRAGACEAE

109. WILD CURRANT or RED FLOWERING CURRANT,
<u>Ribes glutinosum,</u> is a bush with brownish to gray old bark;
leaves round and kidney shaped, dark green above, whitish
below; the deep rose flowers have narrow tubes, the petals
sometimes pale red; berries black, with a bloom. 3-12 '.
First found_____Where_____

110. CANYON GOOSEBERRY, <u>Ribes menziesii.</u> Probably the commonest gooseberry in the area. Young twigs
are densely bristly. Older branches have 3 spines at nodes.
The fruit clothed with bristles; flowers red-purplish, usually very profuse. Plant about 40" high.
First found_____Where_____

107a. Salmonberry (flowers)
(Photo by Violet Wooden)

107b. Salmonberry (berries)
(Photo by Violet Wooden)

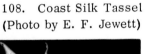

108. Coast Silk Tassel
(Photo by E. F. Jewett)

109. Wild Currant
(Photo by Charles Young)

2. California Aster
(Photo by E. F. Jewett)

110. Canyon Gooseberry
(Photo by Walter Knight)

11. Yellow Stonecrop
(Photo by Violet Wooden)

113. Spice Bush
(Photo by E. F. Jewett)

STONECROP FAMILY   CRASSULACEAE

Rocks
Conif.

111. YELLOW STONECROP, <u>Sedum</u> <u>spathulifolium</u>, has shining yellow, almost star-like blooms held up on tall, thick stems. Sturdy is the word for stonecrops, since they live on rocks both in the mountains and along the sea where winds drag at them. Petals rarely orange or white. 2-12". First found＿＿＿＿＿Where＿＿＿＿＿＿＿＿＿＿

Sea
Bluffs

HENS-AND-CHICKENS or SEA LETTUCE, <u>Dudleya fari-</u><u>nosa</u>, glows handsomely against the weathered rocks above the sea. The little rosettes, each with 14-30 leaves, all densely white-mealy to green; flower stems also white-mealy; flowers pale yellow, sometimes red-flecked. 2-6". First found＿＿＿＿＿Where＿＿＿＿＿＿＿＿＿＿

SUNFLOWER FAMILY   COMPOSITAE

Grass
Mead.
Cultiv.
Brush
Oak
Str. Wd.
Conif.

112. COMMON CALIFORNIA ASTER, <u>Aster</u> <u>chilensis</u>, is a member of the largest of all the plant families. But because we are concentrating on jewel flowers of outstanding interest, we give only one example here. This species shines its lavender and yellow and white flowers in tall ranks along our highways, and even glows brightly through the dust of less frequented country lanes. The flowers extend away from each other by degrees in an open panicle, each flower with 20-35 rays, each 1/4-1/2" long. Plant 16-40" tall. First found＿＿＿＿＿Where＿＿＿＿＿＿＿＿＿＿

SWEET-SHRUB FAMILY   CALYCANTHACEAE

Str. Wd.

113. SPICE BUSH or SWEET-SHRUB, <u>Calycanthus</u> <u>occi-</u><u>dentalis</u>, will surprise you one day as you travel through a mountain canyon, lightly shaded and moist. The unusual blossoms are cinnamon-red in color; the leaves are spicy and aromatic when bruised. 3-19' tall. First found＿＿＿＿＿Where＿＿＿＿＿＿＿＿＿＿

VIOLET FAMILY   VIOLACEAE

Conif.
Brush

114. WESTERN HEART'S EASE or TWO-EYED VIOLET, <u>Viola</u> <u>ocellata</u>, may be found almost all summer long in the

loose duff along mountain trails in the mixed coniferous for-est. The purplish undersides of the petals are strikingly unique in the bud stage, staying deep red-violet on the backs of the two upper petals later; otherwise the petals are white with yellow near the base, the two lateral ones have a small purple eye spot near the base of each. 4-8" tall.
First found_____Where_____

115. REDWOOD VIOLET, Viola sempervirens, is a con-stant bloomer here in the warm area known as the banana belt on the southern Mendocino coast. The creeping plants make a carpet, yellow-starred, in company with calypsos, vancouveria, redwood oxalis, and ginger. They are so gen-tle, small, and demure that the ferns which hover about seem gigantic. The lemon-yellow petals may be faintly purple-veined. Stems lie along ground; 4-12" long. `Conif.`
First found_____Where_____

WESTERN DOG VIOLET, Viola adunca, has purplish red violet flowers, and grows near the ocean. 1-8" tall. `Meadow Conif. Str. Wd.`
First found_____Where_____

WATERLEAF FAMILY   HYDROPHYLLACEAE

116. BABY BLUE-EYES, Nemophila menziesii, is one of our sweetest summer sky-blue gems. It will be found clinging to moist banks, or on protected streams. As its family name indicates, it is a tender plant, but it gladly shares its luminous beauty if treated gently. 4-12" tall. `Grass Meadow Brush Conif. Oak`

SMALL-FLOWERED NEMOPHILA, Nemophila parviflo-ra, is another small, tender plant, but with whitish blooms. `Conif. Oak`
First found_____Where_____

WINTERGREEN or PYROLA FAMILY   PYROLACEAE

117. FALSE PINK ASPARAGUS, Hemitomes (Newberrya) congestum, is saprophytic, since it lives on lifeless plant matter in deep, densely shaded forests. It pushes through the forest floor in masses, each individual flower appearing exactly like an asparagus point coming through the ground. Often the points are roundish, like pink wax lily bulbs, or sometimes rosy red. It is a true treasure. 1-6" tall. `Conif.`
First found_____Where_____

114. Western Heartsease
(Photo by Alice Ackley)

115. Redwood Violet
(Photo by Alice Ackley)

116. Baby Blue Eyes
(Photo by E. F. Jewett)

117a. False Pink Asparag
(Photo by Rolie O'Neal)

121. Indian Pipe
(Photo by Charles Young)

118b. Sugarsticks (jewels)
(Photo by Louise Hallberg)

_eafless Pyrola
by Louise Hallberg)

118a. Sugarsticks
(Photo by Donal McCall)

120a. & b. Prince's Pine
(Photo a. by Ed Jewett, and
photo b. by Wayne Roderick)

118. SUGARSTICKS, <u>Allotropa</u> <u>virgata</u>, are also saprophytic, since they spring up from deep forest duff, in glorious, glistening red and white, looking like Christmas
candy canes, and with green coloring entirely lacking. They
are shown here in two growth stages, but there are other
stages also, and the plants are very long-lived. Beautiful
and rare (because of the foolish people who pick them without thought of beauty's destruction), it is pleasant to find
them even in the fall when they stand in dried splendor, each
jewel-like blossom in miniature perfection. We have seen
colonies of 22, with 2 or 3 of the sticks over 2' tall. 4-24".
First found_____Where_____

Conif.

119. LEAFLESS PYROLA, <u>Pyrola</u> <u>aphylla</u>, is a glowing
gem to find in deep forest. Either alone, or in groups, the
waxy blooms, with red-purple sepals and pink to greenish
petals with white margins, swing up the thick, usually reddish stem like rosy apple blossoms. The style turns downward in the center of each bloom. Exploring the forest
areas at different elevations, we find the early blooming
season at lower levels, but it is a thrill to find the same pyrola species in much brighter colors higher up. 4-8" tall.
First found_____Where_____

Conif.

LARGE WINTERGREEN, <u>Pyrola</u> <u>bracteata</u>, has rose-
purple or dull red flowers, and large basal leaves. 8-16".
First found_____Where_____

Conif.

120. PRINCE'S PINE or PIPSISSEWA, <u>Chimaphila</u> <u>men-</u>
<u>ziesii</u>, is truly winter-loving, or wintergreen, and is a del-
icately-fashioned, low-growing plant, with leather-like and
shining leaves. The perfectly-shaped blossoms appear as if
made of plastic. Showy white or pink blossoms may greet
you along a deep forest trail. Leaves ovate. Plant 3-5" tall.
First found_____Where_____

Conif.
Brush
Hardw.

LITTLE PRINCE'S PINE, <u>Chimaphila</u> <u>umbellata</u>, var.
<u>occidentalis</u>, has pink blossoms and more slender, oblan-
ceolate leaves. It is found on drier, higher ground. 6-12".
First found_____Where_____

Conif.
Brush

121. INDIAN PIPE, <u>Monotropa</u> <u>uniflora</u> (often called
Ghost Pipe). Rare, waxy-white saprophyte; turns black.
First found_____Where_____

WILDFLOWERS BY COLOR

This section is designed to help you identify flowers you see by color if they fit any of the flowers pictured or described in this book. If you find a flower that is purple-red in color, for example, simply look for this color on the list below and turn to the numbered flowers. Flowers not in the color plates but described in the book are numbered as they occur in connection with a color plate flower. Thus 120-2 is Little Prince's Pine, connected with 120, Prince's Pine.

Blue, 8, 11, 15, 35, 46, 47, 51, 52, 100, 116
Blue and Green, 35-2
Blue and White, 24, 116
Brownish, 60
Cream, 68, 74, 75, 78-2, 81, 93, 97, 104
Greenish-white, 49-2   Greenish-yellow, 86-2
Grey, 43, 62   Lavender, 112
Lilac, 63, 64
Orange, 45, 55, 57, 93   Orange-yellow, 59-2
Pink, 13, 33, 37, 41, 44, 48, 56, 61-3, 67, 68-2, 80, 83-2, 95, 98, 117, 119, 120-2
Pink and Purple, 61-3, 80-1   Pink and Rose, 85
Pink and White, 83, 102   Pink and Yellow, 89-2
Purple, 10, 31, 31-2, 50
Purple-green, 7
Purple-red, 28, 49, 85, 91, 93, 99, 107, 115-2
Purple-white, 114
Red, 16, 17, 22, 25, 26, 27, 30, 53, 59, 61, 71, 76, 89, 94, 100, 101, 105, 119-2
Red, Dark, 6, 9, 58
Red-brown, 66, 113   Red and White, 118
Rose, 19, 20, 21, 23, 34, 40, 42, 82, 90, 92, 103, 109
Rose-lavender, 87   Rose and Purple, 49-2, 84, 119-2
Rose and White, 31   Violet, 115-2
White, 5, 12, 14, 18, 31, 36, 38, 39, 61-2, 64, 65-2, 68-2, 69, 70, 72, 73, 74, 74-2, 74-3, 74-4, 77, 77-2, 78, 83-2, 84, 86, 88, 108, 116-2, 121
White-lavender, 2, 98
Yellow, 3, 4, 29, 32, 46-2, 47-2, 64-2, 65, 79, 93, 96, 106, 108-2, 111, 111-2, 115

CONSERVATION OF WILD FLOWERS

Conservation means "wise use." How can that simple statement be improved upon? When we apply the term to our natural resources we automatically think of our watersheds, minerals, forests, and streams. All, of course, are colossal items of importance. But now let us consider a moment the conservation of BEAUTY. How shall this be applied in our ultra-modern world? Shall we start with a fancy hairdo? We are such creatures of conformity that industry thrives as our demands surge upward to reach certain standards of conformity, even in regard to hairdos!

But I think it would be far more wonderful and significant if someone could only be smart enough to induce us all, as parents, grandparents, sisters, brothers, and friends, to strive to keep the stirring BEAUTY of our great outdoors. We especially need to free it of the ugly roadside litter of cans, bottles and other debris of "civilization," and the destructive results of unwisely built roads or fly-by-night lumber operations, and the sick blotting out of beautiful landscapes by garish advertising signs. True enough, there are laws to cover the situation, and signs that plainly state that littering is illegal, yet the "strew-balls" go on with their selfish and fetid work without ceasing.

When sufficient interest on our TV and radio and in our schools and clubs in the preservation of our natural beauties is developed, perhaps the tide will turn. How we pray and hope and work that it will and trust you will join us! A number of interested naturalists, botanists, photographers, and plain wildflower-lovers, like Grandpa Charley and myself, have tried to point the way by carrying litter-bags in our cars to help alleviate the disgraceful debris which so often mars our otherwise lovely scenery. We hope this book will give you a glimpse of the wonderful beauty we can all build if we seek to educate everybody to the need to preserve our wilderness.

Naturalists have different patterns of conservation. One of our co-workers is so interested in every variety of Manzanita that we admiringly call him "Mr. Arctostaphylos," when he isn't around, while another is definitely called "Mr. Fritillaria," and still another is gently referred to as "Mr. Wood Samples." Their contagious enthusiasm is good for us all!

WILDFLOWER SHOWS IN THE REDWOOD AREA

As warm spring showers and sunshine replace chill winter in northern California's Redwood Empire, nature-lovers of this favored region pay annual tribute to its floral glories with a garland of flower shows. Dates may vary with the years, but the following are fairly regular in their order:

1. Last week in April or first week in May.
   BOONVILLE in the Anderson Valley on Highway 128 over toward the coast from Cloverdale. A well-organized community affair is this, showing many of the wildflowers, ferns and shrubs of that beautiful inland-coastal area.

2. First week in May.
   STINSON BEACH WILDFLOWER SHOW, presents California wildflowers, statewide. This is one of the earliest and most popular shows. The location, on the west Marin shore, where roads are lined with poppies, lupine, wild iris, and Indian Warriors, insures a lovely drive.

3. First week in May.
   FORT BRAGG RHODODENDRON FESTIVAL, which celebrates the emergence of the beautiful wild variety of Rhododendron along the Mendocino Coast. These towering shrubs, in brilliant pink and lavender, are easily found by the traveler, since the local Chamber of Commerce establishes signposts for guidance. At this season Simpson Lane, just south of Ft. Bragg, becomes a floral passageway of Rhododendrons and golden Scotch Broom.

4. Mendocino Coast Botanical Gardens at Ft. Bragg and the new Oakland Museum can be visited at any time.

In the southernmost county of THE REDWOOD EMPIRE, San Francisco, watch the paper for dates of various flower shows in THE HALL OF FLOWERS, Golden Gate Park. One of the recognized beauty spots in the entire world is GOLDEN GATE PARK, with its myriads of gardens, always with some flowers in lovely bloom. Wildflowers and their shows are truly the premier jewels in the Redwood Empire's crown.

America's way -- an idea -- cooperation instead of competition among counties -- has brought about the tremendous REDWOOD EMPIRE ASSOCIATION, which has functioned as the promotional leader in this well-known land of the giants, the Sequoia sempervirens, the Redwoods. Born of necessity two generations ago, in 1920, when the Golden Gate Bridge was only a visionary dream, and ferries were the only connection between Marin County and the bay cities, the nine county package consists of San Francisco, Marin, Sonoma, Napa, Lake, Mendocino, Humboldt, and Del Norte Counties in California, and Josephine County in Oregon. All work together as a unit to bring about more and better highways, and cross-country state routes so that you can enjoy our scenic grandeur in safety. For further information direct questions to the REDWOOD EMPIRE ASSOCIATION, 476 Post St., San Francisco, California.

For Wildflower Shows in the wild itself, refer to the maps furnished by any service station or by the Automobile Associations. Many state parks are marked that are good to visit and hunt for wildflowers to photograph, but do not pick them! A rule of thumb to remember is that state and county parks that are found more in the interior and drier places, as among the oak woodlands or savannas or grasslands, will have their wildflower shows for you much earlier in the year than those that are found in the damp and dark redwood forests of the coastal fog belt. When the Pt. Reyes National Seashore is firmly established, it will be a wonderful place to go to see many strange and beautiful flowers, as the influence of fog and wind in this area has produced some unusual forms.

Where you go on private property, be sure to ask permission and be as careful of the wild flowers as you would be in any state park, as the need is overwhelming to preserve and bring back these beautiful gems of the woods and fields wherever we can. How marvelous if we can help make the world more beautiful than we find it!

Congratulations to Mendocino Coast Botanical Gardens, the new Oakland Museum, the California Native Plant Society, the Sea Ranch, and the Independent Coast Observer for keeping preservation of NATURAL BEAUTY in the public eye.

A FEW SUGGESTED WILDFLOWER TRIPS

Stretching from San Francisco into Oregon along California's picturesque coast, the REDWOOD EMPIRE delights the visitor most when its attractions are wreathed in flowers.

Starting in March, flowering cherry trees bloom in the Japanese Tea Garden in San Francisco's 1000 acre Golden Gate Park, furnishing an appropriate beginning for the horticultural year. This event is followed by the San Francisco Spring Flower Show, at the Hall of Flowers - - also in John McLaren's great park.

Then come two blossom tours in Sonoma County - the Prune Blossom Tour at Healdsburg (30 miles through the Alexander Valley to Asti and Dry Creek); and the Apple Blossom Easter Tour around Sebastopol, with its 44 miles of pink-and-white beauty. Thousands of motorists enjoy these tours each Spring.

The Rhododendron Festival at Ft. Bragg in early May (see page 75), features both wild blooms in their natural setting, and cultivated flowers on show in Eagles' Hall. The Garden Society of Marin and the Vintage Festival Committee at Sonoma both stage garden tours in May; and the Luther Burbank Rose Festival in mid-May, commemorates the great naturalist's regard for his favorite flower.

Two notable flower exhibits are the Art and Garden Show at Guerneville in June, and the Marin Art and Garden Fair at Ross over the Fourth of July weekend. A new entry is the Smith River Easter Lily Festival - "Easter in July", held toward the middle of that month in the Del Norte community of Smith River, "Lily Capital of the West."

Fort Bragg presents its annual Fuchsia show late in August, and San Francisco's Hall of Flowers is decked with color for the City's annual Flower Show late that same month.

Concluding the schedule are the Fall Art and Garden Show at Guerneville in mid-September, and the Marin Garden Society's Fall Flower Festival at Ross, toward the end of October. Notable floral displays are also habitual at several of the Redwood Empire's fine county fairs.

ACKNOWLEDGMENTS

Actually it probably all started when our local newspaper correspondent, Mrs. Olga Cossi, chose to picture and publicize some of Grandpa Charley's and my rare botanical finds. Or Jim McNamee and his good wife, Ruth, MIGHT be responsible, since they encouraged us to take some of those same rare specimens to the University of Washington Arboretum in Seattle. Or it could have been Blanche Wilson, who wanted us to go to that fine Wildflower Show in Boonville. Anyway we did manage to share some lovely, rare specimens of Heaths, Groundcones, Orchids and Wintergreens with arboretums, herbariums, and botany departments all the way from Berkeley to Seattle.

It is fun to sit here trying to think up words strong enough to say "thank you!" to the grand people whose pictures have made our DREAM FLOWER BOOK COME TRUE. They are:

Alice Ackley and husband, Merrel, of St. Helena.
Dr. Dennis Anderson of Humboldt State College.
Lula Barnes, Fortuna Color Slide Club, and Lloyd.
The Dr. Paul Bowmans, rhododendron and lily specialists of Fort Bragg.
Louise Hallberg, Registrar, Santa Rosa Junior College.
E. F. Jewett, retired teacher and photographer extraordinary, and Lolabelle, of Fort Bragg.
Christine Kemp, Fortuna. Even though her Frank is no longer with us, I'm sure the beauty he nurtured will live on.
Walter Knight, taxonomist, Tilden Park, Berkeley.
Dr. Gordon McBride, University of Michigan.
Donal McCall, and Mabel McCall of Rio Dell.
Jim McNamee, and Ruth, as mentioned above.
Rolie O'Neal, a good photographer.
Wayne Roderick, UC horticulturist, and his mother, Martha.
Frank Sappingfield, lifelong friend, and his whole family.
Violet Wooden is no longer with us, but her wonderful flower portraits will live forever.

Special thanks go to Walter Knight for this revision, also to his wife Irja Knight, both of Berkeley, Dr. Doris Niles, U. C. Extension, John Thomas Howell, Curator of the Botany Department, California Academy of Sciences in Golden Gate Park, and Barbara and Vinson Brown of Naturegraph for their help.

The following are some books that will be of help in your further studies of wildflowers.

Abrams, Leroy. ILLUSTRATED FLORA OF THE PACIFIC STATES. Four magnificent volumes covering thousands of species, each one illustrated in black and white. Stanford University Press. 1923-1960.

Armstrong, Margaret. FIELD BOOK OF WESTERN WILD FLOWERS. G. P. Putnam.

Baerg, Harry. HOW TO KNOW THE WESTERN TREES. W. C. Brown & Co., 1955.

Clements, Edith S. FLOWERS OF COAST AND SIERRA. Hafner, 1959

Gilkey, Helen. HANDBOOK OF NORTHWEST FLOWERING PLANTS. Binfords.

Haskin, Leslie Lorin. WILDFLOWERS OF THE PACIFIC COAST. Binfords, 1934.

Howell, John Thomas. MARIN FLORA, Univ. of California Press, 1960.

Jacques, H. E. PLANT FAMILIES - HOW TO KNOW THEM. W. C. Brown & Co., 1949.

Lemmon, Robert S. and Charles C. Johnson. WILDFLOWERS OF NORTH AMERICA. In full color; new and very beautiful. Doubleday, 1961.

Munz, Philip A. and David Keck. A CALIFORNIA FLORA. University of California Press, 1963.

Munz, Philip A. CALIFORNIA SPRING WILDFLOWERS. Only lowland flowers. Univ. of California Press, 1961.

Munz, Philip A. CALIFORNIA MOUNTAIN WILDFLOWERS. University of California Press, 1963.

Parsons, Mary Elizabeth. THE WILD FLOWERS OF CALIFORNIA. Edited by Roxana S. Ferris. Dover. 1966.

Rowntree, Lester. FLOWERING SHRUBS OF CALIFORNIA AND THEIR VALUE TO THE GARDENER. Stanford. 1966.

Smith, Gladys L. FLOWERS AND FERNS OF MUIR WOODS. Muir Woods Natural History Association.

Taylor, Kathryn S. and Stephen F. Hambling. HANDBOOK OF WILD FLOWER CULTIVATION. Macmillan, 1962.

Walcott, Mary V., and Dorothy F. Platt. WILDFLOWERS OF AMERICA, edited by H. W. Rickett. Crown, 1964.

PB-02523
5-39
13118-CX
5-39